A New True Book

PHOTOGRAPHY

Written and photographed
By Tony Freeman

*This "true book" was prepared
under the direction of
Illa Podendorf,
formerly with the Laboratory School,
University of Chicago*

CP CHILDRENS PRESS, CHICAGO

Library of Congress Cataloging in Publication Data

Freeman, Tony.
  Photography.

  (A New True book)
  Includes index.
  Summary: Briefly describes the basic principle of
photography, how a camera works, the different types of
cameras and films, how film is developed, and techniques
for taking pictures. Also discusses careers in
photography.
  1. Photography—Juvenile literature. [1. Photog-
raphy] I. Title.
TR149.F86   1983   770   83-7359
ISBN 0-516-01704-7   AACR2

TABLE OF CONTENTS

Uses of Photography. . . 5

Parts of a Camera. . . 10

How a Camera Works. . . 12

Types of Cameras. . . 14

Camera Controls. . . 18

Light and Photography. . . 26

Film. . . 29

Developing Photos. . . 31

Improving Photos. . . 35

Careers in Photography. . . 39

Photography in the Future. . . 42

Words You Should Know. . . 46

Index. . . 47

A professional photographer is often hired to photograph a wedding.

USES OF PHOTOGRAPHY

When something special happens, someone usually takes pictures. The photographer might be your father or mother. A professional could be called to photograph a wedding. You would probably take a camera along on a visit to Disneyland.

Remembering special events is just one use of photography. Cameras are used for many other purposes as well. Some cameras can record things we cannot see with our eyes. An X-ray is a type of photograph that can help a doctor see inside our bodies.

One of the best uses of photography is to carry ideas from one person to another. The photographs in this book do that.

Many people choose photography as a hobby. It is fun to learn how to take good pictures.

Photography exhibit. Often photographers belong to clubs where they share their photographs with others.

People have always
wanted to record what
they saw. Cavemen used
to draw on the walls of
their caves for this reason.
In 1826 a man in France,
Joseph Niepce, found a
way to record images with
light. Photography was born.
Many improvements have
been made in photography

Example of
an early
camera and
photograph

since then. The earliest
cameras needed thirty
minutes or more to take a
picture. Modern cameras
now can freeze action at
one millionth of a second!

PARTS OF A CAMERA

How does a camera work? To know this we have to know how a camera is made.

There are many different kinds of cameras. But large or small, old or new, a camera always has these five parts. Here are the five main parts of a camera:

1. A lightproof box makes sure that the only light reaching the film is light that makes the picture.

2. The film advance is found in most cameras and winds the film from picture to picture.

3. A viewfinder is a device that lets the photographer see what will be included in the picture.

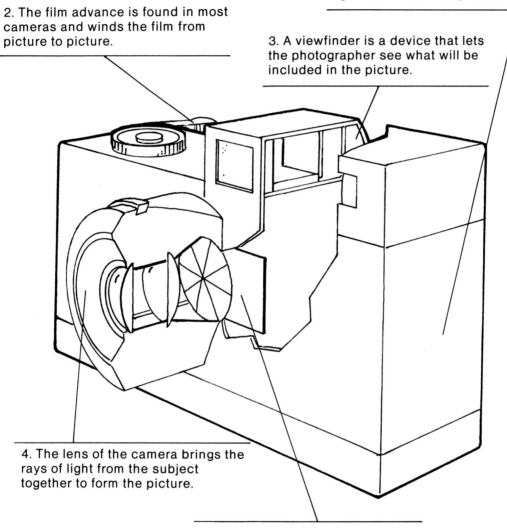

4. The lens of the camera brings the rays of light from the subject together to form the picture.

5. The shutter opens a hole near the lens just long enough to let in the right amount of light. The shutter must stay open longer for a dark subject than for a bright one.

HOW A CAMERA WORKS

When you press the shutter button on a camera, a hole opens to let light in to record a picture on the film. This is called making an exposure.

The light coming through the shutter is made into a picture by the lens. The lens is a piece of glass.

The picture formed inside the camera by the lens is recorded on film.

Cameras use light to record a picture on film. Early cameras
were large and hard to use. Today's cameras are smaller and
easier to use.

TYPES OF CAMERAS

There are four main types of cameras: the viewfinder, single-lens reflex, twin-lens reflex, and the view camera. Each has a special use.

A viewfinder camera has a small window that shows what the camera will include in the photo. Most simple snapshot cameras are viewfinder cameras.

With a viewfinder camera (above left and right) the photographer looks though the window to frame the picture. Single-lens reflex cameras allow the photographer to frame his picture by looking right through the camera lens.

A single-lens reflex camera has a mirror inside that bounces light coming through the lens into a viewfinder. The photo will include exactly what is seen in the viewfinder.

View camera (left) twin-lens reflex camera (right)

The twin-lens reflex camera has two matched lenses. One is for viewing and framing the picture. The other lens puts the picture onto the film.

A view camera is often used by professional

photographers. The photo is framed on a frosted piece of glass at the back of the camera. Light from the lens forms the picture on this glass. To make the picture, the photographer replaces the glass with a piece of film and clicks the shutter.

CAMERA CONTROLS

One of the most important controls is the camera lens. Many cameras allow the lens to be changed. A wide-angle lens includes much of what is in front of the camera. It can be used for scenic pictures.

These two photographs were shot from the same position using a wide-angle lens (left) and a telephoto lens (right). Can you see the deer in the photograph on the left?

Macro-lens photographs of
a flower and a dragonfly

A telephoto lens is like
looking through a telescope.
Telephoto lenses give a
close-up view from far away.

A macro lens lets the
photographer get very, very
close to his subject.

Many cameras can be set for the distance between the subject and the camera. This is called focusing. It makes the picture sharp and clear. Some cameras can be set to focus as close as one inch or as far away as the stars.

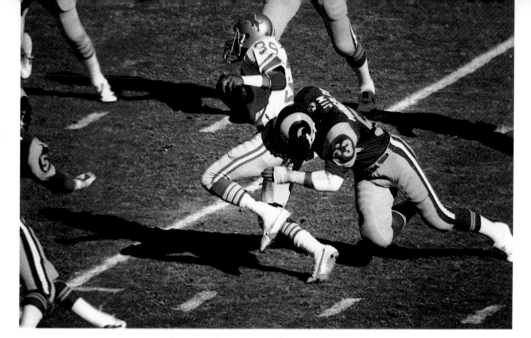

A speed setting of 1/1000 of a second might be used to photograph action during a football game.

The shutter can be adjusted to open and close at different speeds. If it is set to a very fast speed, the camera can stop fast action. Some cameras can be set to click at 1/1000 of a second.

To show movement the photographer has allowed the subjects to blur.

Different shutter speeds can be used to either stop the action or allow it to blur. Sometimes a blur of movement gives a better feeling of speed than does a sharp picture.

Examples of time exposure photographs.

The shutter can be made to stay open for several seconds or even minutes. This is called a time exposure. Pictures of fireworks and buildings at night are made this way.

23

Better cameras have a part called a diaphragm. This is an opening in the lens that can be made larger or smaller. If the light is very bright, the diaphragm is set to a small position. If the subject is very dark, a larger opening is required.

If a large lens opening is used, only part of the picture will be sharp or in focus. If the photographer uses a small lens opening, most of what is in front of the camera will be in focus.

Using a large lens opening (left), only the center person is in focus. With a small lens opening, all three subjects are in focus.

LIGHT AND PHOTOGRAPHY

A photographer needs light more than anything else. Light can come from the sun, a flash unit, or room lights.

There are probably more pictures made in sunlight than any other kind of light.

Sometimes a photographer is indoors and has to be able to move around from subject to subject. A flash unit on the camera makes this possible.

A studio photographer will sometimes use bright lights called floodlights or spotlights. These

Examples of different lighting situations. Natural light (left), using a flash (below left), and floodlights or spotlights (below right).

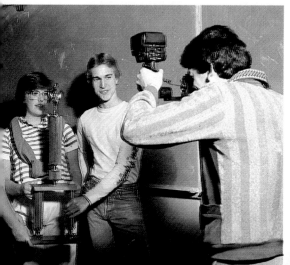

allow the photographer to see what the lights make the subject look like before the picture is taken.

High-speed films are very sensitive to light. They may be used to take photos with normal room lights. Such photos are called existing light photos.

An existing light photograph

FILM

There are two main
kinds of film. One kind is
called negative film. You
can buy black-and-white
or color negative film.
It is used to make prints
on paper. The other kind
of film is slide film.
This makes little color slides.

Instant film can make a
color or black-and-white
photo in a minute or less.
A new film can make
instant slides, too.

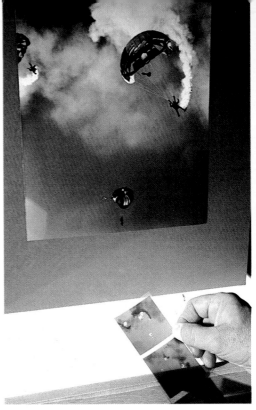

Color slides (above) can be projected on a screen. Negative film (right) can be used to make prints in many different sizes.

Regular print films develop first into a negative. Many prints can be made from one negative. Big prints called enlargements can also be made from a negative.

DEVELOPING PHOTOS

The first step in developing photos is to make the negatives. The film is removed from the camera and taken into a totally darkened room called a darkroom. It is placed in a developing tank that

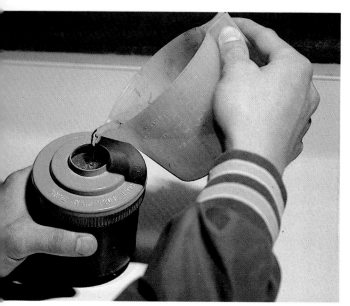

Chemicals are used to process film. In a darkroom an enlarger (right) is something like a slide projector. It is used to make the negative bigger or smaller.

keeps light out. Chemicals are poured in and out of the tank through a special opening. The chemicals make the image appear on the film. It is then okay to take the film into the light.

The most common way to make prints from negatives is to enlarge them. To do this, the photographer projects the negative onto special photo paper with a machine called an enlarger.

The photo paper has a coating of chemicals that react to light from the enlarger. When this paper

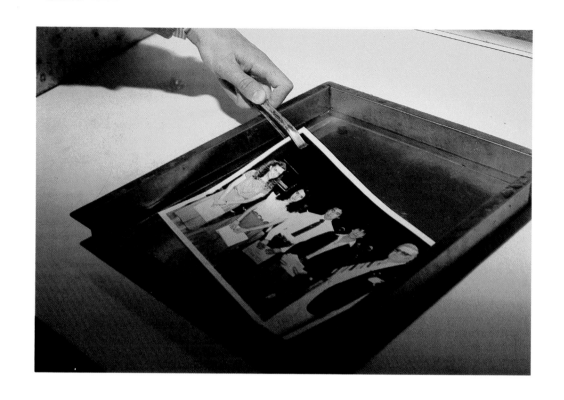

is put into chemicals, a photo appears on it! The paper is usually handled under a special yellow light called a safelight, which does not harm the paper.

IMPROVING PHOTOS

Holding the camera very still is one of the best ways to improve photographs. Many beginners have to learn to hold the camera steady and to s-q-u-e-e-z-e the shutter release slowly instead of pushing it. It is a good idea to practice taking

Keep your camera and lens clean.

pictures with an empty
camera to improve your
steadiness.

Keeping the camera and
lens clean is also very
important. A fingerprint on
the lens will produce a
fuzzy picture even from a
good camera.

The camera and film must be protected from heat. Both can be damaged if they are left in the sun in a car, for instance.

Good photographers often place things at different distances in their photos. This means something will be close to the camera, something a little farther from the camera, and so on. It gives a feeling of depth or distance to the photo.

Some photographers frame their subject. They place their camera so that it looks through an opening that shows around the edge of the photo.

You can improve your pictures of people by showing them doing something.

CAREERS
IN PHOTOGRAPHY

Many people have jobs
related to photography. Some
are photographers or film
makers. Some run
television cameras. Others

Worker develops film.

take X-rays. There are many jobs in photography besides taking pictures, though.

Some people develop film. Others sell cameras

and supplies. Some people
repair cameras. Many people
work in large plants that
make photo paper and film.

Some photographers
work for newspapers or
magazines. Others
photograph only weddings.
Almost all of them have
special training, often
including college courses
in photography.

PHOTOGRAPHY
IN THE FUTURE

New things are being
invented in photography all
the time. The new color
film can be developed and
printed in less than one
hour. A new process
allows color enlargements
to be made in less than
six minutes with only
one chemical. New films
are being made that
allow picture taking with
very little light. Film

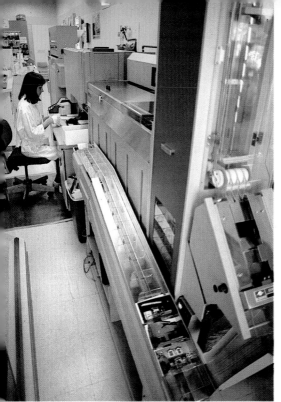

The new films allow photographers to take pictures (above) using very little light. New processing methods (left) have reduced the amount of time needed to develop the film.

cameras are being made to work with television so that photographers can either make prints from their negatives or see them on TV. Photos can be made from outer space that show the weather on earth. Some cameras can photograph the license number on a car from thirty miles out in space!

A photograph can show a breaking light bulb at 1/30,000 of a second. Entire jet airplanes are checked by huge X-ray photographs.

Photography is a language
that is all around us.
Even the words in this book
are produced with the help
of photography. It is almost
impossible to go anyplace
where photography has not
been used to make something,
to carry ideas, or to make
our world more beautiful.

WORDS YOU SHOULD KNOW

diaphragm(DYE • ah • fram) — an opening in a camera lens that can be made larger or smaller

exposure(ex • PO • jure) — to record a picture on film

flash unit(FLASH • YOO • nit) — a light that is used with a camera to take photographs

focus(FO • kuss) — to adjust a camera to get a clear image

frame(FRAYME) — to look through a lens and decide what you want your photograph to include

image(IM • ihje) — the picture formed on film

lens(LENZ) — a shaped piece of glass in a camera

macro lens(MACK • ro LENZ) — a lens in a camera that allows you to get very close to what is being photographed

negative(NEG • ah • tiv) — an image on film in which the areas that are usually light are dark and those that are usually dark are light

print — a photograph made from a negative

process(PROSS • ess) — a series of steps in developing a photograph

record(ree • CORD) — to take a photograph of a subject

sensitive(SENSS • ih • tiv) — able to respond to light easily

shutter(SHUT • er) — a part of the camera that opens to allow light in when a picture is taken

single lens reflex(SING • il • LENZ • RE • flex) — a camera that views through its lens. Single lens reflexes are usually selected because lenses are easily changed on them.

telephoto lens — a lens on a camera that brings the subject close

transparent(tranz • PAIR • ent) — to be able to see through

twin-lens reflex — a camera that has two matched lenses

viewfinder(VYOO • fine • der) — a camera that has a small window which you look through to frame the photo

wide-angle lens — a lens on a camera that allows a wide area view to be photographed

INDEX

black-and-white film, 29
blurs, in pictures, 22
cameras, 5, 6, 9, 10-25, 26,
   35-38, 40, 41
cameras, controls, 18-25
cameras, earliest, 9
cameras, holding steady, 35, 36
cameras, how they work, 12
cameras, keeping clean, 36
cameras, parts of, 10, 11
cameras, protecting from heat,
   37
cameras, types of, 14-17
careers in photography, 39-41
cave drawings, 8
chemicals, 32-34, 42
color film, 29, 42
controls, camera, 18-25
darkroom, 31
depth in a photo, 37
developing photos, 31-34, 40
developing tank, 31, 32
diaphragm, 24
distance in a photo, 37
earliest cameras, 9
enlargements, 30, 33, 42
enlarger, 33
existing light photos, 28
exposure, 12

film, 11, 12, 16, 17, 28, 39-31,
   33, 37, 40, 41, 42
film advance, 11
film makers, 39
flash unit, 26
floodlights, 27
focusing, 20, 25
framing a subject, 38
France, 8
future photography, 42-45
glass, in view camera, 17
high-speed film, 28
hobby, photography as, 7
improving photos, 35-38
ideas, carrying by photography, 6,
   45
instant film, 29
instant slides, 29
lenses, 11, 12, 15, 16, 17, 18,
   19, 24, 25, 36
light, 11, 12, 15, 17, 24, 26-28,
   32, 33, 43
macro lens, 19
mirrors, 15
negative film, 29
negatives, 30, 31, 33, 43
Niepce, Joseph, 8
parts of a camera, 10, 11
photographers, 5, 17, 26, 27, 39, 41

photo paper, **33, 34, 41**

prints, **29, 30, 33, 43**

safelight, **34**

scenic pictures, **18**

shutter, **11, 12, 17, 21-23, 35**

single-lens reflex cameras, **14, 15**

slide film, **29**

slides, **29**

space, photos from, **43, 44**

special events, **5, 6**

spotlights, **27**

studio photographer, **27**

sunlight, **26**

telephoto lens, **19**

television, **39, 43**

time exposure, **23**

twin-lens reflex cameras, **14, 16**

types of cameras, **14-17**

view cameras, **14, 16, 17**

viewfinder, **11, 15,**

viewfinder cameras, **14**

wide-angle lens, **18**

X-rays, **6, 40, 44**

ABOUT THE AUTHOR

Tony Freeman has taught photography at the high school and university level for more than twenty years. His students have earned many honors with their photographs in contests and displays. Many of them have gone on after school to become professionals in many different areas of photography.

Freeman has written many magazine articles about photography. For over a year he wrote a question and answer column for a national photography magazine. He answered many questions that were sent in by readers of the magazine.

He has been active in the National Photography Instructors Association and was president of this group at one time. He is the winner of the C.A. Bach Award presented to the most outstanding photography teacher once a year.

Freeman has six children and all of them are also very much in love with photography. It is this love of photography that Freeman enjoys sharing with young people that caused this book to be written.